Leonard Bernstein

T0061346

Psalm 148

Soprano and Piano

Archive Edition

LEONARD
BERNSTEIN
Music Publishing
Company LLC

BOOSEY & HAWKES

AN IMAGEM COMPANY

DISTRIBUTED BY
HAL•LEONARD®
CORPORATION
7777 W. BLUEMOUND RD. P.O. BOX 13819 MILWAUKEE, WI 53213

www.boosey.com
www.halleonard.com

Published by Leonard Bernstein Music Publishing Company
Boosey & Hawkes, Inc., Sole Agent
35 East 21st Street
New York NY
10010

www.boosey.com

 an IMAGEM company

First printed 1993

Psalm 148

Words adapted by the composer

Leonard Bernstein
(1935)

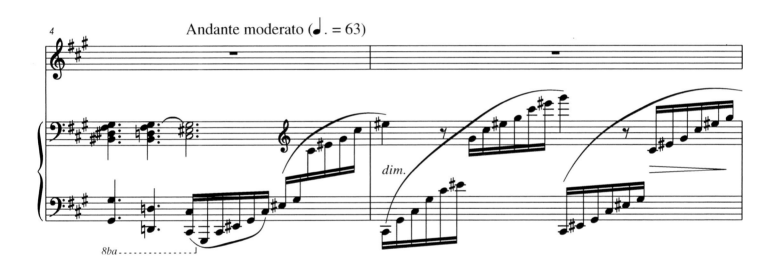

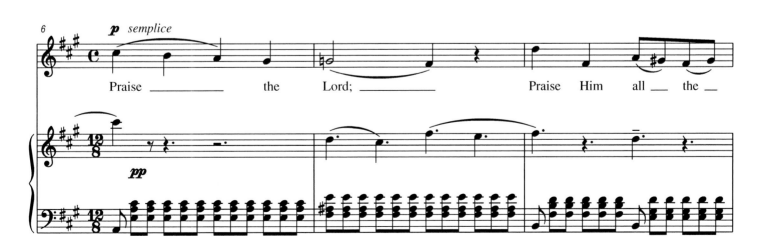

Praise _____ the Lord; _____ Praise Him all __ the __

Printed in U.S.A. 1993

Tempo Primo (Andante)

U.S. $16.00

ISMN 979-0-051-93440-9

ISBN 978-1-4768-1338-7

LEONARD
BERNSTEIN
Music Publishing
Company LLC

BOOSEY & HAWKES

DISTRIBUTED BY

HL48022320

Elliott Carter

La Musique

Solo Soprano

HENDON MUSIC

BOOSEY & HAWKES

DISTRIBUTED BY

HAL•LEONARD®

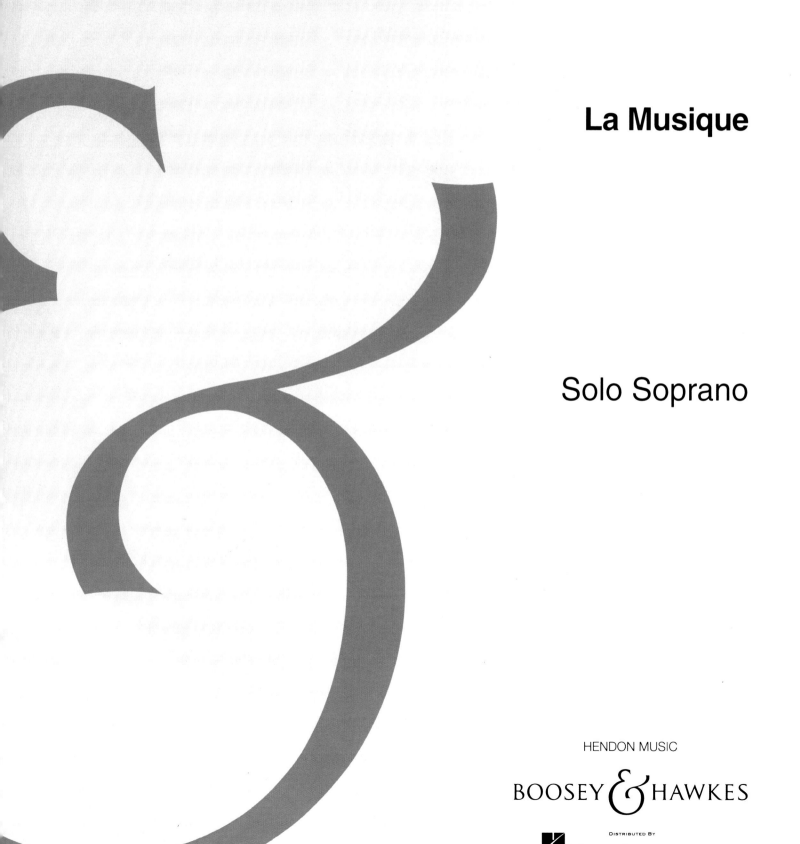